SUSAN BROWNE
ZEPHYR

PRAISE FOR ZEPHYR

If I'm lucky,
I'll have dinner tonight

surrounded by friends at the table,
our hands sculpting air,

trying to say how living feels.

There you have it: the precise reason why I read poetry. Again and again Susan Browne's poems sculpt the page and the air, telling us in ways both beautiful and funny how it feels to be alive in our strange selves in our strange, exuberant and entranced times. How can you resist someone who so freely admits, I'm not that good a person / and I know it's true / because I don't feel that bad about it"? Who wishes she were more spiritual, "but belief is like making your cat / wear a sweater"? I can think of few poets who mine so movingly that dark chasm between pathos and humor, which is where America seems to find itself these days.

—GEORGE BILGERE

The poems in Susan Browne's *Zephyr* are grounded in the mysteries of this terribly known, outrageously funny and sad world. With an expert sense of language and narrative, this intrepid poet cranks her highbeams to rummage "humanity's basement, the murk inside the mammalian heart" and unearths each dark, radiant truth.

—DORIANNE LAUX

Susan Browne's *Zephyr* is an exuberant collection, as entertaining as it is heartfelt. If you think life on earth is absurd, meaningful, unbearably beautiful and downright awful all at once, you've found the right book. Browne is a witty and skillful chronicler of the "mortal ugh" in which "God is the pizza guy" and "you're not thankful enough, / you don't put your shoe on your head enough." I for one am thankful that "this once world" now contains this fine second collection. I plan to try the shoe thing, too.

—KIM ADDONIZIO

ALSO BY SUSAN BROWNE

Buddha's Dogs

SUSAN BROWNE

ZEPHYR

STEEL TOE BOOKS
BOWLING GREEN, KENTUCKY

ISBN 978-0-9824169-4-5

STEEL TOE BOOKS
Western Kentucky University
Department of English
1906 College Heights Blvd. #11086
Bowling Green, KY 42101-1086
steeltoebooks.com

AUTHOR PHOTOGRAPH
Tina Humphreys

COVER AND BOOK DESIGN
Molly McCaffrey

Who has seen the wind?
Neither you nor I:
But when the trees bow down their heads,
The wind is passing by.

—CHRISTINA ROSSETTI

For Kenneth

CONTENTS

O N E

IF NOT NOW, WHEN?

You wake to the birds' heavy metal
and the knowledge that more people are killed
by donkeys than in plane crashes.

You read this last night and it's stuck
in your brain, part of your Toxic Thought Syndrome,
like pondering how twenty-five hundred
left-handed people are killed annually from using
right-handed products.

You get up and do a few laps in the coffee pot.
Can coffee kill you?
Consciousness, your own personal guru,
watches Mind, like the sky the air, observing turbulence.

Like everyone else's, most of your thinking is repetitive.

At your desk, you roll up your sleeves,
and write another poem about death:

We came home from the hospital, sat in the family room.
Dad cried into the couch, then said,
"Mom's never been dead before."

You don't feel like making a transition
to the next stanza because you don't have 3,000 years.

Your sister talks to her husband's ashes
that are in a black enamel box on her dresser
between the Eternity perfume bottle and a dish of earrings.

"Hello, Dearie," she says in the morning on her way
to the shower, and in the evening, curls up on
the bed and discusses her day.

Finally, after two years, her children convince her to scatter the
    ashes.
She doesn't want to carry the black box in the golf cart,
too conspicuous, no cremains allowed on the fairway,
so she asks your advice, but a Glad Bag is wrong.
She decides on Tupperware.

Where does the soul go when the body dies, asked Aldous Huxley
There is no necessity for it to go anywhere, answered Jacob Boehme.

You met God when you were nine years old.
You rode your bicycle up the hill behind your neighborhood,
stood in the mustard weed and listened to the eucalyptus
    leaves clapping.
The sky swallowed you and you swallowed the sky,
orange and pink and you brimmed
with ecstasy and grief. Then you came down the hill for love.

Besides Aldous, there are only four words in the English lan-
    guage that end
in dous: stupendous, tremendous, horrendous, and hazardous.

Even if someone shoots you in the head, don't take it personally.
After all, thirteen people are killed annually by vending machines
falling on them.

At any one time, 0.7 percent of the world's population is drunk.
This seems like an unbelievably low estimate.
The average person laughs fifteen times a day.
This is not enough.

Your sister phones, says she hasn't had any hot dates lately.
Actually, she hasn't had any. She's kind of sad this week
because it's almost another year of Dave being gone,
but she's going to a party tomorrow. This is life,
she says, and she has to pick it up a notch.

You don't ask her the Zen question: What, at this moment, is
    lacking?
You say, Let's go shopping for strappy shoes.

ZEPHYR

The father wants to be loved, but so does gum.
Look at the way it sticks to your shoe,
and for miles of tumbleweeds and deserted husbands,
it won't come unglued. You could go barefoot,
you could turn into a zephyr, but wherever you roam
the father or something like him finds you. Clump, clump,
one leg shorter than the other, one bumpy mile closer
to the airy insubstantial. Who wins?
Everything will happen to us is written across our precious
grudges. There are choices like sand or dandelions,
and they blow away into the sea. Meanwhile, you can make
a castle with a moat around it, or a salad with flowers.
Choose. I love you, I love you not.
The traffic lights aren't changing, they're afraid
you'll never get any further than yellow.

ON OUR FIRST DATE

He ordered oxtail, heap of dark meat
he scooped with his hands off the white plate,
saying, *The marrow has the best flavor,*
but while eating, he didn't talk, he gnashed and gnawed,
he chomped to the bone, sucked and swallowed,
chin glinting with tail juice, mouth gleaming with gristle,
fingers growing thicker, meatier, and when he finished,
I wondered if he'd lick the linen tablecloth
where a gelatinous dribble had dropped,
I hadn't touched my poached salmon, fork raised,
ready to use as a weapon against this animal dressed in jacket
and trousers, his silk shirt splattered with braised sinew
and blood, he finally looked up, *Do you like your dinner?*
O *yes,* I said, and he smiled, his teeth wet from plunder,
from long submersion in the body of another.

KING OF THE WILD FRONTIER

I'm so young, I wear my Davy Crockett coonskin cap all day,
and won't take it off, not even when I go to bed.

I'm so young, I wonder if maybe Davy was a girl
like me before becoming King of the Wild Frontier.

I'm so young, I adore my crazy parents who drink
water and olives out of wide-mouthed laughing glasses,

who dance and sing, and my father calls me the dog's name.
I'm so young, I chase next-door-Tommy with a spoon

into his house and smack him on the head until he bleeds,
and my head's bleeding, too, where he hit me first with the
    spoon,

and we both scream and scream, and our mothers can't stop us.
I sit with an egg on my head on Tommy's porch

the next morning, waiting for him to come outside so I can
see his egg, and we'll play buckets and anything with sand.

I'm so young, there's nothing better than the palm tree's hair
swish-swishing green in the blue breeze and salt on my skin

mixed with sunshine and fudgcicle.
I'm so young, I never think of God,

but the day I almost drown,
I know the dark sea loves me.

LIFE IS TOO HARD

is the first sentence I read when I'm finally in bed
after driving for five hours in a rainstorm,

after the funeral of my brother-in-law.
I nod at the sentence like an old friend, and down a paragraph,

again at A *major disadvantage to living is death*, then realize
I'm reading a satire and start chuckling, quietly

because I'm next to my husband who is sleeping like the dead
after working sixteen hours, so I tap him on his arm,

and he flinches, and my heart returns to its normal labor,
but when I read, *Why we were brought into the world only to suffer
     and die*

is an area of research in which much remains to be done, I laugh hard,
practically falling on the floor, holding my stomach,

my shoulders shaking, and wander through the dark rooms
of the house chortling and hiccuping, bumping into a chair

that looks different, lumpy and dented, and where is the end
     table,
did we throw it out? Something is missing, something is wrong.

I sit on the couch, hunched over as if I'm still driving through
     the rain.
My brother-in-law will not be here again, ever.

In the bathroom, I stare at the towels that need to be washed, laughing a little between gasps in order to stand it.

FIRST DRINK

Valerie and I were only going to take a sip
from the bottle of tequila Jeff Hudson
had stolen from the Pierson's garage
and hidden behind the bleachers, just one
little swig for two little tipplers
sitting on a bench, dressed for the dance,
bows in our hair, the green pool of the football field
shimmering in the sun still high
in the sky as I slammed my first taste back
which came right back up, but I wanted to know
the alchemy of alcohol, the lushness of liquor,
the buzz of booze, wanted to get drunk as a skunk,
plastered and hammered, tanked and stewed,
sozzled and soused, pie-eyed and plowed,
it was my birthright, my bloodline, my DNA,
so with the strength of generations, I kept it down.
I said to my friend, "Let's have another,"
and we passed the bottle around until
the field was drained and the sun went blind,
the worm turned white and the seraphs arrived,
each with three pairs of wings, then four then five,
swinging and singing and flying
us so far out of our minds our bodies levitated
and finally landed in our respective backyards.
I lay on a chaise lounge, bow tilted, head toppled
toward the vomit while Mother yelled,
Who the hell did this? And I didn't say
I did it myself, it was awfully fun.
The next day I stood at the fridge

with an unquenchable thirst,
I would do it again,
I would have another and another,
I had not learned my lesson,
it had just begun.

AGAIN,

disturbed by my own behavior, so disappointed, thwarted
by being so human, or maybe it isn't human, or if it is,
it's humanity's basement, the murk inside the mammalian
    heart—
I could have counted silently, breathed, meditated,
kept my hyena mouth shut, but instead
I asked the woman beside me in the packed theatre
to please turn off her cell phone, which rang
two different times, and I thought she did,
her hands fumbling around, but it rang again,
so then, my God, she was old enough to know better,
she was about my age, I commanded in a superior whisper,
"Turn that phone off now," but, again, it rang,
and the woman stared straight ahead, so I aimed
my voice like a weapon at her stricken, pale face
and said loudly, "What is your problem?"
and then felt sick with rage and guilt
because the way I said it sounded like
you are a dumb stupid idiot,
and she bumbled through her purse again,
and the green light flashed on the little phone screen,
and she looked at it like she just had to
know who was calling, and that did it, I yelled, "Jesus,
you're an idiot!" and got up and almost fell down
the stairs, rolling over spilled popcorn
trying for a fast get-away, blurting, "Idiot, idiot"—
and did the mother penguins return safely from the sea,
the babies survive, I cried seeing how they helped
each other, huddling in a huge half-frozen clump

as I march alone down the cold street,
hitting myself in the head with my flippers, imagining hundreds
of penguins with cell phones ringing in the endless arctic
night, I'd want to shoot those gabby featherbellys,
blast them off the tundra, I should move to the desert,
but the point is to live with people,
I give up, I'll try again, and I wonder how that woman
is doing, she coughed a few times and sneezed,
I hope she's okay, I hope she wasn't contagious,
maybe she was waiting for the one call
her son or daughter could make from prison
or the army, but she missed it,
and now she's all alone, I'll take some vitamin C
when I get home, and if I had her number,
I'd call her.

MANDOLIN

Rain like soft bullets on the roof under which I don't sleep,
thinking about cruelty as subtext, thick and sickly courteous
as marmalade jam laced with polonium-210, the scintillation
    cocktail
given to Litvinenko. Be careful at work, be vigilant about who
    would prefer
you dead. It's easy to kill a person and unfolds in the flesh
    like a series
of bureaucratic steak knives. I wish I liked drugs more, I wish
    I could take
a sleeping pill, but even Dayquil makes everything look like a
    postcard
bought in a bus station with nothing behind it except stale air.
I wish I were more spiritual, but belief is like making your cat
wear a sweater, or having sex with your socks and flannel paja-
    mas on
although I'm jealous of the nonviolent faithful and wonder
    whatever happened
to the pale blue cross that used to hang on the wall above my
    childhood
and adolescent pillow. Every night I prayed to little gold Jesus,
saying one *Our Father* and one *Hail Mary* and blessing every-
    one
until I didn't so much stop as forget, too busy with familial
    fear
and dread. I used to be nicer, I used to cry more.
I wish I didn't live only once, I need more practice.
Each morning, I should wake up, saying, "I died last night."
Remember when we sat in the bar, and while I complained,

you sipped your martini, then pointed behind my head.
"What? What?" I asked. "Look! Look!" you said.
I stared at rows of bottles backlit and glowing,
they made me giddy, all that possibility, but they were only bot-
    tles.
So?" And you said, "The world didn't have to be here
but is." If I had to have a religion, it'd be you. Do you still
    want to
hammer another nail in your father's coffin? My soul is five
    parts mandolin
and two tin whistle and not for any planetary reason; it's fur-
    ther away
and deeper. Today the clouds are dark blue with a furious
gold splitting the seams. My friend lives in a hospital bed,
and her lover wheels her into the living room so she can see
    more
stuff and it's brighter. For six months, a balloon lived
in the pine tree outside my bedroom window. It was green
    and tender
and kept me company while I did sit-ups. And then the wind
    came,
but in its absence, I see it.

YOU'RE NOBODY TILL
SOMEBODY LOVES YOU

When you're alone,
the bed is the North Atlantic,
the floor a shatter of sharks.
Why walk all over each other?
Once I threw a small vase
of petunias at the mortuary wall.
What have I learned?
To keep comforting crushed marsupials.
Here, have a petunia.
It's still beautiful, even with
a few cracked ribs.

THE NOSE ON YOUR FACE

In all your life, you will never see your actual face.
If you close one eye, you can gaze
at the side of your nose, but that's it.
Is that why when looking at group photographs,
it's yourself you stare at the longest?
Sometimes you're mistaken for someone else,
And you want to meet her, see for yourself yourself,
but even if you met a gang of doppelgangers,
you will continue searching in hubcaps, sauce pans,
toasters, the backs of spoons, the bases of lamps,
in sunglasses, in another person's eyes,
and if that person is standing in just the right light,
there you are, trying to get closer.

TWO CLERICS HACKED TO DEATH
IN HOLY CITY

I just love that, so let me say it again.
The alliteration alone is admirable, and the cadence—
nothing better than iambic pentameter:
Two Clerics Hacked to Death in Holy City.

Man, that's got swing, ring-a-ding, and an action
verb. I can really feel it, *hack,* I can almost see it,
hack, hack, hack. Talk about a wake-up call.
This morning, I'm reading the news, checking in
with the war when like music to my ears:

Two Clerics Hacked to Death in Holy City.
It should win the Pulitzer, or maybe
the Nobel. But then I turn the page,
and listen to this:

A Five-Year-Old Aims his Kalashnikov.
Such lovely triple rhythms! A natural progression,
and I can't wait to hear tomorrow's song:
the harmonics of humanity, the croon
of carnage in every holy city.

ALONE IN PARADISE

Leave us alone
drinking the good wine,
savoring the whole fish stuffed
with fennel and sweet onion,
wheels of lemon juicing its silvery scales.
Leave us alone at the white, wrought iron table,
listening to the cicadas while the lagoon's green chemise
turns gold in the huge doubloon of moonlight,
leaving the dishes for the maid
and mamboing across the marble tiles.
Who wants to think about those who hate us
so much they would gladly kill themselves
to kill us? Leave us alone as we shut off
the news, select a new cd, dvd,
light jazz, a romantic comedy
and unchain the pit bull,
activate the security system,
lock the electronic gate,
position our nuclear missiles,
erect a shield over this hemisphere,
protecting ourselves from the hell
of the rest of the world.

GET OUTTA DODGE

Tomorrow is another war
Followed by a cloud with a plutonium lining,
And pessimism can only get worse,
So it's better to cut your heart out.

Cheer up! Every rose has its dynamite,
While what doesn't kill you
Will serve you succotash.

Have another round. La via esta duro, amigo.
Here's to the darkest dawn at the end
Of everything relative,
And bling bling healing all things, except the universe
That shall inherit nonbiodegradable worlds.

IBIS

I feel that jobs are unnatural for me.
I've always been more inclined to gaze
out the window at fence whorls, imagining
a cinnamon puma crouched in the acacia.

Who will pay me to observe the world deeply
and make a few surprising comments?

To witness aurora borealis in porch lighting?

What can I say right now that's worth
the money I need to live,

and why should I receive this honor?

Why is the scarlet ibis flying over the crematorium?

TO THE MOMENT

Thank God you're here,
eternal warrior who wrestles against the joyless
onslaught of mortal ugh.

I want to be in you more—what else is there?—
like waking at dawn and listening with my skin
to the wet animal of the ocean. O rambunctious me

into wave-crashing light. I want you today
and tomorrow, definitely tomorrow, don't forget
about tomorrow. I'm yours, and so far you've been loyal

if not always pleasant like being whipped into a dither
by the cerebral yakety yak of the species in seminars
and committees, but O how large foreheads shine

like apples and how lovely the shy flutter of smudged
glassed-in eyelids toward each other.
I'm honored to be your witness, moment,

even watching my father weep in his lonely house
the morning his second wife didn't wake up,
and then I stood on the lawn and waited for the coroner,

while an ice cream truck chimed along the street.
Sometimes I think you're crazy, wondering what
you'll do next, but I have to trust,

and I love your lulling side
like when I lie in bed after afternoon sex
with my sweetheart, his snore in my ear,

the cat glaring if we dare move. Or when a friend
and I settle in at the best seat at the bar, and that first sip
of cold wine, and then the menu and the sumptuous

decision about pommes frites or ruby jewels of beet salad.
O, moment, you're not toujours gai, but often enough for me.
I'm sticking with you in shiver and shudder

wherever you're going, great yogi, you who doesn't mind
what happens because everything happens. We'll have it all:
simmery coq au vin, satiny halibut on top a tangle of clams

as the darkening skylight fills with mandarin orange.

FAIRY TALE ELEGY

Once upon a time in the Land of Sad,
a girl went on a journey.
She was not a princess, except to her mother,
but her mother was dead, killed by three dragons:
Depression, Despair, and Destiny.
Her father had vanished some tipsy moons ago,
kidnapped by the pirate Captain Smirnoff.

The girl packed her knapsack
and set sail to the land of colorful fishing boats
and stone churches, Stations of the Cross
staining the windows.

At Communion, she covered her face
with her hands as her mother had taught her.
She lay on a hotel towel on the beach
and drew patterns for dresses
that curved in at the waist
and would make her look like a princess
though her mother would never sew them.

One day the girl almost drowned in a riptide,
but she quit fighting,
and the waves brought her back to shore.

A week later, she met a man
who braided her hair. They drank red wine
on the roof of the pensione
and watched laundry on the line

move in the dark wind.
The girl wished she could love him,
but she had to return to the Land of Sad.

She went to her mother's grave
and made a wish to stop being angry,
to grow up now and feel at peace.

Autumn came, then winter.
Three springs passed
before she met a good witch
known far and wide for her healing arts
who lived in a cottage with a Zen garden,
Karma Cleaner in calligraphy on the mailbox.
This was obviously in Berkeley.

Everything would change.
The girl would meet a Prince from Denmark,
not Hamlet, but he'd have a few dozen problems
like everybody else.
At first kiss, the spell would lift,
the iron wheel turning.

But not yet.
Not yet.
It takes a lot of work to break the curse
of the Land of Sad.
Happily-ever-after is as hard to find
as a needle in Rumpelstiltskin's straw.
You must learn how to spin what's given
into the gold of yourself.

HARD TO BELIEVE

We stood by our mother's grave
in black silk sheaths.
She taught us to be stylish
whatever the occasion:
death or gardening or playing poker.
My younger sister couldn't afford a dress
so had bought one at Nordstrom,
a store known to take everything back.
As the priest intoned the valley of the shadow,
I whispered in my sister's ear
that the white sales tag was flagging out
from her armpit.
Then our father climbed into the grave.
His best friend, Mad Dog,
nicknamed for what he did
in the war and in bars across the free world,
grabbed a handful of suit coat,
saying, "Get outta that trench, Bobbie B."
The dew on the cemetery grass
glittered like diamonds.
My mother loved diamonds,
her birthstone, brilliant and hard.
When she discovered she was dead,
she'd say, "I could spit bullets."
I wanted a God, not fuzzy light
At the end of a tunnel,
someone kind and funny for my mother,
a mixture of the Dalai Lama and Dorothy Parker.
I was waiting, though, to see the coffin lid slam open

and my mother rise up, yelling,
"No way, José!"
We threw the weird, wilted roses without thorns
on the beige casket.
I imagined my mother demanding to speak to the manager,
"Beige? Are you out of your mind?"
wanting another color, a different style,
or she was going elsewhere.
After the funeral,
my two sisters and I linked arms, walking carefully
in our high heels across the shimmering blades
of East Lawn Mortuary.
Sometimes, when I look in the bathroom mirror,
I see my mother rummaging around in the drawer
for her eyebrow pencil, mascara, and rouge,
asking, "Where's my face?"

REPORT

My head is full of interstellar marbles
    surrounded by a magnetic field indirectly spawned
by the gaping black hole at the galactic heart
    as I try to fathom Jesus' face appearing on a pancake in Ohio

although one account said it was not as authentic as the Virgin
    Mary discovered on a grilled egg sandwich in Florida
that was kept partially eaten in a plastic box
    on the nightstand of Diana Duyser for ten years

until she sold it on eBay for 28,000.
    Do you ever feel like laughing or weeping uncontrollably
or howling your head off when someone tells you
    life is short or asks for directions?

In a dream, the lawn was a trampoline, and I jumped so high,
    I sprang out of the earth, it was magnificent,
but I missed zinfandels and hurricane sunsets,
    the wants of wanting, pedicures, everyone

I can't believe I'll never see again, yet it's part of rapacious desire:
    the cancer reproduces itself, the terrorist makes his point.
Do you ever wonder, *when will I unpack my orphan suitcase,*
    let go the sad satchel of unborn love?

It's been reported: luminous strands of darkness
  are twisted like a double helix of DNA
across the center of the Milky Way, like you and me
  and my lost dog who twenty years later,

I still sometimes think I see, riding in the back of a truck,
  wolf's head tilted, mutt lips curled
in the wind as if she's grinning,
  fur rippling in sunlight like black fire.

TWO

SADNESS

You wanted to be happy
but got hooked on sadness.
You could be sad
while watering the lemon tree
with your tears,
while husking corn for cornballs,
while brewing saccharine tea.
You could be sad all by yourself
or among a crowd of people,
which really made you sad
because there were quite a few humans
you didn't want to be with,
but you were often lonely
and this was a doleful enigma
causing a downhearted dysphoria,
burying the joybones ten thousand leagues deep.
The only solution was to play sad music
and gnash your cornballs
in order to keep your strength up
for more sadness to come.
Every once in a while you smiled,
but that was over when your lemon tree croaked.
Sadness was yours to have and to hold
from each day forward into doom.
Your one hope was to be the saddest person alive
and win an award. The Blue Ribbon of Despair.
It would be a fierce and despondent competition,
and if you lost, you'd be depressed.
But you won, and now you mope around
cheerfully inconsolable.

THE DEPONENT'S TESTIMONY

The lawyers sat in their dark suits.
I swore to tell the truth.
You had just died in a car wreck.
The stenographer took notes.

I swore to tell the truth.
We were suing for wrongful death.
The stenographer took notes.
The tire on your car was faulty.

We were suing for wrongful death.
Depositions are a discovery tool.
The tire on your car was faulty.
They wanted to discover how much your life was worth.

Depositions are a discovery tool.
Did your mother smoke?
They wanted to discover how much your life was worth.
Did she drink alcohol?

How many cigarettes a day did your mother smoke?
This was a civil litigation.
Would you consider her an alcoholic?
Would you consider her a good mother?

This was a civil litigation.
I asked them to stop.
You were a good mother.
I stood in the hallway and wept.

I asked them to stop.
You had just died.
I stood in the hallway and wept.
The lawyers sat in their dark suits.

LAST THINGS

When I got home from work,
I saw the blinking red light,
But I walked by the phone
On the little antique table in the hallway.
My mother had given me that table.
In the kitchen, I stared at the cupboards.
Food was a thought although I wasn't hungry.
It could be a long evening was another
Although time would stop.
I knew something had happened,
And I didn't want to know it.
I went to the store, don't remember what I bought.
Cooked, ate, washed the dishes,
Put on my coat. I pushed the button,
Heard my brother-in-law's voice, *accident.*
My mother was in surgery, I should call this number.
I looked out the window. There was nothing to see,
Except a dark wind.
On the way to the hospital,
I passed the mangled median divider,
The crushed chrysanthemum bushes
Where the police would find my mother's purse.
I drove toward my mother's dying.
The moon shone cold and clear on the concrete.

ODE TO LILY JEAN

for my niece

Here by the sea and its urgency
I think of you, pure urge
pushing out of your mother's body,
the amniotic wave of you,
the salted scalp, the glistening black kelp
of hair, the exquisitely squinched crabby face of you
hanging in the tangy air, and the slick shoulder
shouldering out a briny arm, a starry hand,
you appear as if from the sea of nothing,
swimming into pure, oceanic you.

GRACE

Things have been a little easier since I realized God
is the pizza guy who's been standing at the oven at Dopo

for the past three years in His tomato splattered apron,
shining His teeth at me when I pick up my phoned-in-from-
    the-freeway

dinner, beaming like I'm His pizza acolyte, even though we've
    never spoken
and my hair resembles bubbled cheese or melted anchovies.

When I see His loopy grin lassoing across the greasy air of exis-
    tence,
I think, *now that's grace,*

He doesn't care about sin or salvation, He's just glad to see me
filling the hungry space between us.

I give Him my sweetest smirk as the pie is passed like a com-
    munion wafer
over the altar of the counter, and I walk lightly

down the street of my town, over one hundred murders this
    year and counting—
what's the deal with suffering?—

in a universe discovered by scientists this very day to be a vast
    trampoline
made up of tiny vibrating loops of string like mozzarella.

DRIVING HOME

I drive home the winding road way,
gripping the wheel, singing at blind curves.

The street looks like liquid mercury,
& time's a colorful blur.

My first memory is of dying. It sort of helps.
When I was three, I almost drowned, unafraid,

tumbling with anemones, their funny tentacles,
among drops of sunshine.

Fear was on shore, life burning
in my chest again as I choked on air, saved.

Sky darkening now, clouds shaped like gargoyles.
The radio newscaster announces the traveling circus

of catastrophe. If I'm lucky,
I'll have dinner tonight

surrounded by friends at the table,
our hands sculpting air,

trying to say how living feels. Then we'll bow
over warm food, cold wine, the fleeting

fragrances of ideas & ease & plans.
Wherever I am, I'm still listening

to when the story began
with my parents & sister in a love bungalow

on Lanai Street, to the waves carrying away
the sand, to a parrot swearing in Spanish.

I drive on, through the valley, wishing I had faith
in something besides melancholy although

sometimes I feel as calm & sacred as that cow
grazing sideways on that hill in this perilous wind.

DUSK

That time again, the surrendered sky,
    calligraphy of branches and leaves,
crickets soothing the silence
    with their leathery song,

and I watch darkness come
    as I have for 22 days, here
in the country of the sick
    while October turns,

    and my body turns, flu to pneumonia.
Deep in my bed like a chrysalis,
    I wait for night to pass, for breath
to unfurl its wings and lift me

though I know, too, everything tends toward darkness.
    I've had long hours to remember the dead,
trembling for where they've gone—
    We did what we could, but, the doctor said—

feeling the disbelief which can't be
    disbelieved, until you also go
and don't return, and maybe not
    even then.

A friend told me once
    he didn't believe in death.
When he died, there was a party,
    as he'd requested, instead of a funeral.

Sometimes he used to irritate me,
   always cheerful, always playing
bebop music and shouting, *Bella!*
   this and *Bella!* that

as if the world were only beautiful.
   I remember his car, dented like a can,
colorful serapes covering torn seats,
   Frank Sinatra crooning out the window

that wouldn't roll up.
   He brought me lasagna,
badly painted pictures,
   odd gifts in strange boxes.

He always wore a hat: beret, fedora, sombrero,
   or a yellow scarf with elephants
dancing around his head.
   No such thing as death, he said.

And yes, he lives
   inside my healing form,
in the horizon still clearly defined
   in this scattering light.

A ROBIN WITH RAGGED WINGS

perches on the edge of the roof, chirping feebly
to the sky, his head turned at an odd angle
as if his neck is broken, and some of his feathers
look like the cat tried to saw them off
with her claws. He's about to die any second,
but he doesn't stop his song,
reminding me of the many on earth who ask
and never receive. I stand by the window,
wondering how can I help, searching the apple
tree for his buddies to come save him.
I go outside for a closer look. He's gone.
The yard is weirdly quiet without
that wretched singing.

TUESDAY

The front door's smashed open, wood busted,
Hinges broken, a dusty space
Where the TV had been,
And what you feel is Oh.
Not a matter of if but when,
As in when you die everything will go.
The new camera bought for the vacation,
Gone. On the table the empty Olympus box
With the warranty, now you don't have to fill out
The little cardboard form, the flimsy guarantee.
In the bathroom, you're stunned to see
The strand of pearls still on the counter—
You put it on, put on another necklace,
Bracelets, rings. In the bedroom,
Your underwear scattered across the floor.
Then the police arrive, their radios blaring.
Sorry, they say, but this happens every day,
Oh, you say. Just Oh, nodding, wearing all
Your best jewelry at once.

SUMMER VACATION

snorkled in toxic water between the crossings
    of glass bottom boats loaded
with tourists from four cruise ships anchored
    like floating skyscrapers
in the bay blocking the view of the coastline
    then climbed into a motorized polyurethane
raft crammed with scuba tanks stun guns soda cans
    saw one bald eagle
on the one scorched square mile of cliff left
    without condominiums
and the assistant guide to the guide said the bird is
    tagged *see the orange splotch*
use the rubber armor tripod adaptable multi-coated binoculars
    we take the egg out of the nest and fly it
to San Francisco non-stop hurry up incubate
    and replace it with a fake egg
and when the bird hatches jet the baby back drugged
    in a locked box look! dolphins
they're leaping away from us but don't worry
    we'll follow get real close

HUMUS

After working with people all day
and driving home surrounded by people,

we relax in the evening with people
and watch television shows of people,

many of them working, driving,
and watching television shows.

When we go to bed,
hopefully with another person,

we read a novel about people.
Deep in the night, we dream of people

who are supposedly ourselves.
In the morning, we can't wait to check our email

to see if someone left a message.
Home from work again, we race to the mailbox,

yearning for a letter from none other
than a person.

On the weekend, we go to a movie
and, among wall-to-wall people, stare at people on the screen.

The bars and restaurants are crammed with people
to eat and drink with and, hopefully, at least one person

to go to bed with.
In school, sociology shows us how people live,

biology explains how people reproduce,
and psychology guesses how people think.

Archaeology studies ancient people's skulls and jawbones
and the first fork people invented.

At the grocery store, we stand in a line of people,
reading *People* magazine.

Many people attend church on Sunday.
A popular belief is that after we die,

we come back as people.
Another favorite notion: we go through a tunnel of light,

and at the end, who's there to meet us? People.
Forget God. There are people.

PERSEVERE

How come my silver platter is a paper plate
wiped for re-use after the picnic,
and where's the reward for these teeth,
how they shine while being drilled? How dare I
ask for points, no one scores for living.
You have to kneel down
on all fours and work like any goat
gnashing through steel. See? We're talking about you again,
what about me got crunched. Stop complaining, I tell my self
as self cries, "I never get the wombat
I deserve." Wombat says, *what about me, I don't even have a tail.*
Perhaps lack is karmically earned
and serves when diving into burrows to escape
Dingos and Tasmanian Devils. I'm growing
cartilage, a tougher hide for the cosmic combine's
cuts and threshes sanctifying the grain.
It's a field of ouches out there,
but after the yadda yadda of surviving,
where's the gold-starred Band-Aid? Nevermind.
Eons haven't stopped my trajectory
from a flicker of Precambrian meteorite.
And I appreciate the long line of ant sandwiches.

FORGIVE

So much was forgiven today.
The night forgave the dawn
For stealing the stars.
The weeds forgave the gardener
For yanking them out at the roots.
The fence forgave the ivy
For breaking its slats.
Amanda forgave the cop car
For almost hitting her head-on,
Chasing the bad guys
Who the good guys,
If they're really good,
Will have to forgive.
Sometimes you have to pretend
So much of your life didn't happen
To manage another day of forgiveness,
Or to stay in the same room
With that special someone
You wish would fall off a cliff.
Did forgiveness begin with the nightmare
When you were a child
Of being stabbed in the back,
The knife going through your heart
And into the mattress? Your parents
Sat with you in the living room,
Just a dream, they said.
Let the soul forgive its sadness
As you crash through the opening into this world,
As you set out on your journey, crushing
The earth beneath your feet.

AT BLOOMINGDALE'S GRAND OPENING
IN SAN FRANCISCO

I can't find my way out
of the new shopping center
which was added on to the old shopping center
and now covers two million square feet of earth.
I explore orbits within orbits of excess,
wandering the labyrinth of plethora,
lost in the Land of Glitzy Gods
gilded in leather and spandex,
platinum palm pilots jewelling their hands.
"Why are you so rich?" I ask the man standing next to me
in the mall's marble-floored, silk-walled, chandeliered bar.
"Finance," he says, shooting down
six Kumamoto oysters with a double flute
of Cristal. Dollars birth dollars,
shopping centers birth shopping centers.
The world is a bank within a store within a mall within a big-
    ger mall.
I can never go outside again,
these doors only open onto other doors,
down into the funnel of more and more,
until I'm buried in denim, ten thousand different kinds of jeans,
a cross made of diamonds driven into my heart.

MOUNTAIN

Maybe a map is a good thing
On those days I feel
Like I'm riding a rhino up a mountain,
Looking for the door in the cloud.
Is there an outline for fate?
When is it due?
My heart is numinous
When it's not bituminous.
I'm not that good a person
And I know it's true
Because I don't feel that bad about it.
What a relief to face the sword
Of myself mirroring how steely
My smile, how sharp my desire,
How I would cut anything down
To keep on moving.
Sometimes I want to surrender
So completely, I would be nothing
But a drop of sweat in a rhino's eye
As he clambers up and up, thirsty
And without complaint.

THREE

LISTEN

One day I won't think I'm so lucky,
and I'll realize how lucky I was
like today, driving home in traffic after the Russian roulette
of the mammogram, and the driver behind me going 110
misses my car by a half-inch, and the police have cordoned
off the lanes containing the mattress and the bucket,
and the leafy green July world looks like an arugula salad,
the light like Dijon mustard drizzling through the branches,
and I'm hungry for the earth
because I don't live enough in it while I'm living.
I want to forget my heart's amnesia,
embrace my breath's insomnia,
staying awake all night without me, breathing in more
of this life than I'll ever smell or taste or touch,
and I wish I could see myself sleeping, or your face
when you don't have your face on,
when you're alone and loneliness has bloomed into
a giant broom and swept clean every corner of self-pity.
I love us then like the early morning walk we took
in an unknown city, the sky like a blue egg
balanced on high dark walls,
the broken fountain with its few shining pennies.

ON OUR ELEVENTH ANNIVERSARY

You're telling that story again about your childhood,
when you were five years old and rode your blue bicycle

from Copenhagen to Espergaerde, and it was night
and snowing by the time you arrived,

and your grandparents were so relieved to see you,
because all day no one knew where you were,

you had vanished. We sit at our patio table under a faded green
umbrella, drinking wine in California's blue autumn,

red stars of roses along the fence, trellising over the roof
of our ramshackle garage. Too soon the wine glasses will be
        empty,

our stories told, the house covered with pine needles the wind
has shaken from the trees. Other people will live here.

We will vanish like children who traveled far in the dark,
stars of snow in their hair, riding to enchanted Espergaerde.

ENOUGH

You're too serious and not serious enough,
you're not thankful enough,
you don't put your shoe on your head enough.

A student, Mandeep from Calcutta,
walks with you to your office,
giggles in the doorway,
then solemnly recites Tagore.
She's the reason the day isn't dust.

Night, the glass of wine,
the rose blooming in the cactus tree outside,
Kenneth in bed, asleep, bruises stamped under
his eyes from too much work.

Dark sound of leaves shaking in the dark.

You wish, you want—

Enough!

You could touch more, you could move your hands more
and keep moving,

a slow wind all over his body.

In the middle of the night like leaves shaking.

HOT FLASH: TWO A.M.

I'm lying in bed, my body grinding its worn out
Reproductive gears, and I toss and turn
And shiver with sparks, my dry eyes stuck to their lids,
I'm thirsty, I want to throw myself in the sea
To feel outside what used to be inside, so tired of incinerating,
So I wrench my eyes open and stare at the moon waning
In the window, halfway gone like me if I live
To be one hundred and six, and I remember
A man saying, *What's it like to know you are Paradise?*
And at the time I thought what a dumb line,
But now it's brilliant, where is he,
Where are those men who couldn't get enough,
And I wish I'd said yes
To every slobbering one of them, drench me
With kisses, and I take my husband's hand
And put it on my breast, *You're so hot*, he says and yawns,
Yes, I say, turning to him like a wave
Burning wildly, mortally.

FACING FIFTY

I like my wrecked face, etched
with the trenches of my life,
and when I laugh, they turn into rivers,
the battles washed down to the sea.
I have never been so old or ugly,
I will never be as beautiful or young.
After rubbing Oil of the Inconsolable
underneath my Vaudeville eyes,
I hurdy-gurdy in the mirror
like a ten-year-old girl
who could care less.

ELEGY FOR MY FLANNEL PAJAMAS

Tonight, I'm wearing them for the last time—
they are nearly sheer from years of washing, the roses faded—
lying in bed under the print of Chagall's lovers
floating around the ceiling of the Paris Opera.

The lovers aren't wearing anything
except pink and green swirls of paint, gliding
past the Eiffel Tower, the Arc de Triomphe,
and a smiling horse with a curly mane,
both eyes on one side of its head like a flounder.

I hope in the afterlife, my lover and I
float in afterglow, selves worn to transparency,
hearts transformed into invisible roses,
doves chuckling in the turquoise myrtle trees,
God like Chagall, flourishing his brush, saying,
"Only love interests me."

I turn off the lamp and sleep like the dead
until my love comes home and sits on the edge
of the bed, unbuttoning my pajamas.

ON A LINE FROM MILLAY

What lips my lips have kissed, and where, and why,
could fill a small atlas with Greek kisses
and French kisses and Oakland and San Francisco
kisses, and I can't forget the Dublin kiss
that lingered in its wreath of Guinness,
which brings the kiss of longing for kissing in rainy
doorways, the melancholy kiss like wind
through leaves. This once world kisses only
here. Kiss me, dear Ephemera.

LITTLE WISHES OF AIR

for Kim

Whatever stalks the yard at night goes home to sugar and milk.

Your mother safely crosses the street.

Your brother's liver is a miracle of distillation.

Love is not aka are you insane.

August rain rinses the leaves, opens the scent of wild grape.

All appointments with death are cancelled,

Along with your credit card debt.

LIVING IN KYOTO

Even in Kyoto—
Hearing the cuckoo's cry—
I long for Kyoto

              —BASHO

I run on the path behind my town,
drooling dogs pawing at my legs,
moms trudging behind strollers,
babies wearing little lumpy canvas hats
and looking imperiously cranky
like *When will I grow up and get out of here?*
While I wonder *When will I grow up and get into here?*

This is it. Earth's the place to be, there being no other,
so I follow the baby posse's trail of cookie crumbs
past the blue dust of eucalyptus leaves,
October's gold falling on thistle and poison oak.

I want to live longing for Kyoto
while I'm in Kyoto, for the shine
on the rock on the side of the road,
for the light inside everything,
even sorrow.

SKOL

September light, watery gold,
fills up the glass of the world.

Just played tennis: dried sweat, relaxed flesh—
blissed at the old patio table,

listening to leaf blower, feeling like balsa wood,
like I'm the holiest person I know.

LET US LIVE ONLY FOR PASSION,

for the taking off of clothes,
tossing them over our shoulder,
let us live to step out of our underwear
and wear it on our heads while dancing
to *Jumping Jack Flash*, let us live for laughter
as I shimmy up and down the lamp pole,
as you fling yourself back and forth against the wall switch
creating a light show, your penis gleefully flapping,
let us not live for appearances, let us kiss
and kiss and kiss until we vanish
into kissing.

WHAT A BEAUTIFUL DAY
FOR A HANGOVER!

When I wake, I can't open my eyes;
they're sealed shut with tequila.
Thus I lie scanning for illumined thought,

but lids suddenly smack into brows, so I jangle up
and carry my body like a cracked egg into the kitchen,
knowing today I'll never rise

to any occasion other than an omelet.
Besides four aspirin, vitamin B-complex, and an icepack,
heavy remorse:
this evening, tea for penance.

In the bathroom, I almost unmanifest
when I see how good I look for how bad I feel,
proving the spirit is greater than the flesh,

and outside, the air blazes with blue dakinis,
so I collapse in a lawn chair under the wild rose bush
to practice omphaloskepsis,
as mystics have for centuries.

ODE TO AUTUMN

Thoughts are mist. I'm restless,
yet tired as an old leaf. I yell at the yellow trees,
I see you! See me!

The light going to dark, a friend in the hospital, surgical
saw slicing his cranium, then what, radiation, chemo.
Pour another glass of wine, cook that salmon, it's fake,

farm-raised, good although something dangerous in it,
you could investigate but why
be completely clear about semi-edible poison?

We're cleaning out our basement, gleaning
for the holidays, searching the furrows of ornaments
for the cardboard skeleton to hang on the door.

Things multiply, ooze out of their cells. Plenty more
to replace everything. Have you noticed the ripening
of drill bits, cars, jeans, medical plans

few can afford. O, we go like leaves,
a wailful cliché however it happens,
lost cricket in the hedge-row, bleating lamb.

I glare at the mystery until I imagine
sitting on death's branch, gazing out on rooftops
hours by hours, the rosy-hued peace,

the sky reflected in the neighbor's pool.
Climb down through a melancholy choir
of gathering gnats and pow, it's blue,

sun igniting water. Then cool cement,
and drowsy perfume of woodsmoke, just-cut
grass. Close your brimming eyes,

hear your heart's soft treble,
until you're lifted like a rain drop in reverse
into the tattered pearl of a winnowing cloud.

THE LAST DAY OF THE YEAR

On the last day of the year, I throw 2008 in the trash.
The calendar is crumpled from falling off the wall; by December,

eleven pages of months have been hanging around long after
their moment in the sun, all bunched up and shivering

behind Ansel Adams' photograph of Yosemite Valley buried
under pounds of snow. The little squares of days are now at rest,

no more doctor's and dentist's appointments,
no more root canals, cancer scares, English Department
    meetings,

the year collapsed in on itself, 365 black holes added to the
    cosmos
of newspapers, yogurt containers, and wine bottles.

Staring at the empty space on the wall, I'm soothed by utter
    blankness.
Nothing to look forward to, nothing to look back upon.

No yearning, no remembering. As if God pushed the Pause
    button.
A shiver shoots down my spine, and I think about getting a
    new calendar,

on January 2nd when the stores open, and the machine of the
    world
cranks up again. The world of things

to do, little squares of days in the sun, a table, blue flowers in a vase, a menu, a glass, a plate.

ACKNOWLEDGMENTS

Grateful acknowledgment is made to the editors of the following publications in which these poems, or versions of them, first appeared:

"Mandolin": *Subtropics*, May, 2009

"Zephyr": *Subtropics*, May, 2009

"Report": *Margie*, finalist, 2008, Best Poem Contest

"On Our Eleventh Anniversary": *Mississippi Review*, April, 2007, finalist for the poetry prize. This poem is also published on Ted Kooser's *American Life in Poetry* column, 2009

"Again": *The Comstock Review*, Fall/Winter Issue, 2006

"The Last Day of the Year": *Smartish Pace*, Issue Thirteen, April, 2006; second place in the Erskine J. Poetry Prize Contest

"First Drink": *Never Before, Poems about First Experiences*, Four Way Books, 2005

"If Not Now, When?": *River Styx*, 71, 2005; first place in the *River Styx* International Poetry Contest

"Two Clerics Hacked to Death in Holy City": *Margie*, Volume Four, 2005. This poem is also published in

Ordinary Genius, A Guide for the Poet Within, by Kim Addonizio, published by Norton, 2009

"Life is too hard": *Ploughshares*, Winter, 2003-04

"Hard to Believe": The Emily Dickinson Award Anthology, 2001, Universities West Press

Thank you to Kim Addonizio and Karen Toloui for advice and comments on the manuscript.

Thank you to Tom and Ralaina Hunley for Steel Toe Books.

Thank you to my family for always love.

Born in Long Beach, California, SUSAN BROWNE has lived most of her life in the Bay Area. Her first poetry collection, *Buddha's Dogs*, won the Four Way Books Intro Prize, selected by Edward Hirsch. Her poems have appeared in *Ploughshares, Subtropics, River City, The Mississippi Review, Smartish Pace,* and *Margie.* Her awards include prizes from the Chester H. Jones Foundation, the National Writer's Union, the Los Angeles Poetry Festival, and the *River Styx* International Poetry Contest. She teaches at Diablo Valley College.

CPSIA information can be obtained at www.ICGtesting.com
Printed in the USA
LVOW08s0253100516

487498LV00001B/22/P